MOM IN SPACE

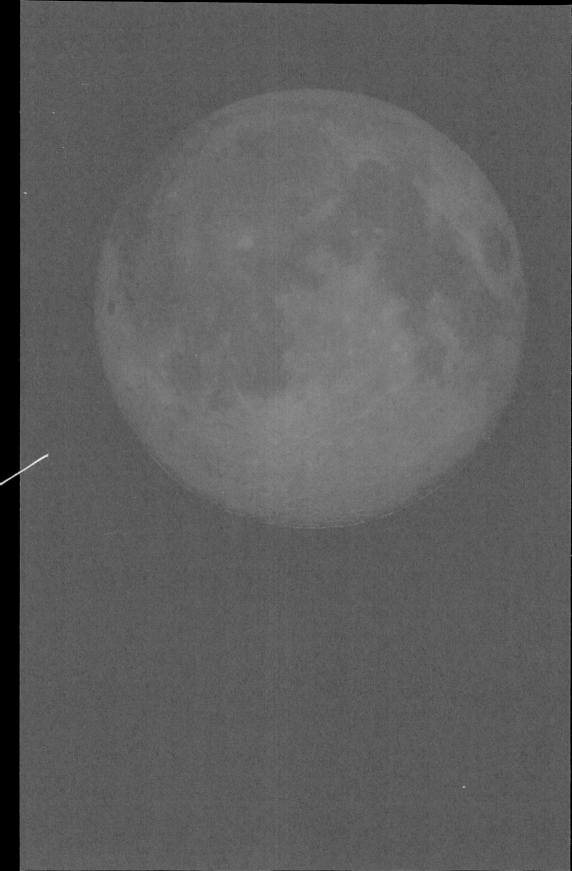

MOM IN SPACE

POEMS

LISA AMPLEMAN

Louisiana State University Press   Baton Rouge

Published by Louisiana State University Press
lsupress.org

LSU Press Paperback Original

DESIGNER: Barbara Neely Bourgoyne
TYPEFACE: Sina Nova

COVER PHOTOGRAPH: From the series *The Lonely Astronaut—
Green Suit Edition,* by Karen Jerzyk, 2018.

Images of phases of the Moon courtesy NASA/Bill Dunford.

Library of Congress Cataloging-in-Publication Data
Names: Ampleman, Lisa, 1979– author.
Title: Mom in space : poems / Lisa Ampleman.
Description: Baton Rouge : Louisiana State University Press, [2024]
Identifiers: LCCN 2023025166 (print) | LCCN 2023025167 (ebook) | ISBN
    978-0-8071-8125-6 (paperback) | ISBN 978-0-8071-8159-1 (epub) | ISBN
    978-0-8071-8160-7 (pdf)
Subjects: LCGFT: Poetry.
Classification: LCC PS3601.M73 M66 2024 (print) | LCC PS3601.M73 (ebook)
    | DDC 811/.6—dc23/eng/20230526
LC record available at https://lccn.loc.gov/2023025166
LC ebook record available at https://lccn.loc.gov/2023025167

At night I lie awake
in the ruthless Unspoken,
knowing that planets
come to life, bloom,
and die away,
like day-lilies opening
one after another
in every nook and cranny
of the Universe,
but I will never see them [...]

What sort of woman can it be
who feels at home
in all the Universe,
and yet nowhere on Earth,
who loves equally
what's living and ash?
    —Diane Ackerman, "Pluto," *The Planets* (1976)

What are you doing? Oh, you're writing words down
and then reading them. Boring.
    —my son, age 5

Space never ends—even if you go infinite miles, it keeps
going on. Space grows every millisecond. You can only
go beyond it if you go where it's being created.
    —my son, age 7

Contents

MOM IN SPACE

LUNAR DECEPTIONS

"Genetically, all women are mosaics." In utero, the double X chromosomes need paring: we can't have the same gene expressing twice. So, some genes turn off, allowing their parallel to do the work instead. But "in certain cells, the X chromosome inherited from the mother is inactivated, while in other cells the X chromosome inherited from the father is inactivated." The XXs glimmer differently, prisms that can't quite mirror each other exactly.

Under the steady shine of the harvest moon, I lie to my pajamaed son, tell him Mars is a star, because he wants to wish on "The Wishing Star" and none are visible. I'm trying to get him to bed on time. It's just a fib.

Of course you've heard that women's menstrual cycles sync up with the stages of the Moon. In a study of twenty-two women, some did show alignment. But night owls bathed in artificial light never synchronized, and one researcher notes that when we lived in a darker world, women who were pregnant or breastfeeding "had perhaps 40–50 cycles in a lifetime—which means there was not much opportunity for … syncing with the moon."

The Moon causes our ocean tides—but it's not that simple. The water in a backyard pool doesn't lift up toward the full moon, whose gravity is anemic. Instead, in the "liquid body" of the interconnected oceans covering 70 percent of our globe, each molecule pushes on others, under the influence of the rotating, gravity-heavy Earth. When the Sun's force comes into play too, we get spring or neap tides.

In the school drop-off line next to the parish cemetery, my son wants the harvest moon still full in the pink western sky to be closer, so he can see the astronauts. "Are they real?" he asks, meaning every cartoon has an episode with fictitious star-travelers, a challenge overcome. He knows already some things we tell ourselves are just pretend. I try to explain low-earth orbit and budgetary restraints as we idle, some grave plinths and monuments seared white by the Sun on their eastern edges. We make lists of *O* words: oak leaf, on/off, outside, and my mind keeps spawning them after he's wriggled out of the car: overcast, octave loosely linked to its sestet, ovary smooth without the scars of age, doling out its largesse while it lasts.

The Moon is not an *O*; it has a tail dragging behind it, irradiated sodium catapulted from the surface after meteor strikes. Every month, during the new moon, Earth wears the tail "like a scarf." My son does not believe this tidbit because he cannot see it. And anyway, that morning Moon can't be the real thing, must be a projection, as convincing as the soundstage where they filmed the landings, too sublime to be real.

If women trying to conceive want to align with the Moon, they can try lunaception. Sleep in complete darkness for two weeks starting with the new moon, not a hint of light in your room. Get blackout curtains, cover your alarm clock, eschew night-lights. Then, turn on a dim lamp while you slumber, for three days in a row (this is your fertile period). Then, during the waning moon, back to the darkness. When you've tried everything else medicine has to offer, this might seem like a reasonable, affordable option.

Eighty percent of those with autoimmune issues in the U.S. are women. One theory: the differing X chromosomes brim with immune-related genes ready to mutate, or the X prism-sisters don't recognize each other and form antigens to their kin. And in pregnancy, a woman's immune system squelches the urge to destroy foreign bodies, is weakened and primed for mismanagement.

Or maybe we just don't have enough babies these days. The placenta communicates with the immune system, fine-tuning how it works. In those times with darker nights, when women were pregnant much of their adult lives, that placenta regulation happened often enough. Our bodies evolved to expect it. But if we're not constantly bearing children, without the intervention of the placenta, the immune system gets confused and aggressive, "starts looking for things to attack that aren't dangerous."

I didn't meet my husband until I turned thirty, then we struggled to have children, then we had one. Then we miscarried, struggled to have more. I've spent only forty-eight weeks of my life pregnant. Then I developed an autoimmune arthritis. Sometimes, now, I'm relieved I don't have to parent-through-pain more than one child. Sometimes.

The goddess of the Moon, Selene, drove a two-horse chariot. She loved a mortal shepherd, Endymion, and asked the gods to help him slumber eternally so she could visit him nightly. In one version, she bore him fifty daughters, the number of lunar months between Olympic Games. If the sky was dark, she was at his white-rocked cave with him, perhaps conceiving.

Nixon's staff prepared a speech in case the Moon landing failed, words that ring false now: "They will be mourned by a Mother Earth that dared send two of her sons into the unknown.... In their sacrifice, they bind more tightly the brotherhood of man.... For every human being who looks up at the moon in the nights to come will know that there is

some corner of another world that is forever mankind."
Mother, sons, brotherhood, man, mankind. A Mother full of
children, far from other worlds. Her own enclosed sphere, in
which well-intentioned warriors attack what seems foreign
but isn't.

Sometime later this decade, a woman will step onto the
Moon. Her menstrual cycles will likely be suppressed to
avoid complications. She might not be allowed as much time
in space over her career as male astronauts, since the risks
for radiation cancer are higher. She might be a mother. XX
chromosomes will shimmer prismatically in her cells. We'll
see her presence there as a foretold legend. She will lie to us,
out of kindness: *It's worth all the sacrifices,* or *This feels like
home,* or *I wish you all could be here with me.*

REASONS FOR LACK OF SUCCESS

The BPA saturating
grocery-store receipts
    or sprayed into cans
before the chickpeas and beans.
    Genetic defect,
a stripe of helix miscoupling,
    glitch written as my
genesis coded itself.
    Pestilence or
pesticides as I lolled
    in the womb. Too
much time in hot
    tubs or not enough,
chronic stress,
    the grime that gathers
around the bathroom fixtures
    no matter what cleanser
I try. Adhesions
    from my appendix:
peritoneal snarls.
    A closed soul,
not wanting a child
    with the fervor it deserves.
Wanting it excessively,
    posing together like a nativity
set without its centerpiece,
    out of season,
sentimental. Like that
    insect that entered
through the exhaust fan
    chirring at the window:
bamboozled by biological urge.

BILLBOARD

It's not the billboard people's
        fault. They speak to those
who need a lustrously lit hospital room
        with faux hardwood

in which to birth their babies. *New*
        beginnings born here, and a happy couple—
regular folk, not impossible models—
        gazes at their little sack of blankets,

their miraculous tangle
        of recombined DNA.
Perhaps you should tell
        the billboard people

to be more sensitive. After all,
        you flamed the insurance company
that kept inviting you to their "Moms Club"
        even as they billed you

for the miscarriage. There is no
        Empty-Cradle Club.
If there were, the code of conduct
        would be *Say nothing*

to friends and family, avoid
        spreading the disappointment.
And over time, members would
        drop out slowly,

disappearing before they start to show,
        leaving the folding chairs
filled with the inveterate.
        You can recognize them

by the half wince, the blankness that
        takes over their face
when a pregnant woman enters the room:
        something has been sucked

out of them. The marrow of any possible joy.

THE THREE-YEAR-OLD IN THE
FERTILITY-CLINIC WAITING ROOM

declares he's
        Superman, swoops
to the trash can,
        scrambles onto
a chair and tramples
        a magazine
as he stomps
        his feet, nearly
losing a sandal,
        jubilant in
his defeat of
        the villain,
is shushed by
        his flustered mother
as she tries to fill in
        in an endless form,
hurtles from
        end table to
brochure rack and
        back again, skids
to a stop below
        the pastel floral
wall, the video
        screen that
alternates between
        a rosy baby
and examples
        of payment plans.
Imp, you are
        an aberration here.

Nonhypothetical,
        noisy, you are what
we bystanders
        do not hope
and hope for.

BARREN TRINKETS

Each calcite cave-pearl clanks against its neighbor,
the *what-if* eventually connected to the *no-never*.
Eat one—swallow it so it can gestate or fall
apart in your stomach. Approximate gem.
Like a candy necklace, sweet circle
by circle, the chain dissolves over enough
time, leaving you without options,
though you can pretend you chose.
Each imagined child is a talisman, Catholic scapular
rubbing your neck, piece of felt you must keep
in good repair. No, not that easy—they're
the shrieks on the wind, a playground
a half mile away and cradled in the valley's acoustics.
Use these topaz earplugs to stop the noise.

TENUOUS BLUEPRINT

> The way things work
> is that eventually
> something catches.
> —Jorie Graham

Speck of a specimen, mite of a maybe,
iota of an outline, every nucleotide
ready to sequence & seam,
to grow something or power it off, certified

and approved, curled in double
helix, your start & perhaps
your end encoded in the jumble
of enzymes. Phoneme, syllable, syntax:

the advance is staggering. Split
& multiply, cells. Poppy seed, peppercorn,
blueberry. Mystical sewing kit
and the garment itself to be worn.

Whatever you do, keep dividing. Keep
reconnecting. Heart, hip joint, cheek...

BIRTH

The rocket-powered vehicle trails umbilicals
        snapped loose by its climb,
cables, pipes, and hoses that rivered in—or
        drained—hazardous gases,
arm that connected the White Room to claustrophobic
        pod. Oh explosive bolts, thunk subtly
in the hullabaloo of the engines.
        Dear shear pins—shaved off as the launch system

rises, unhurried—be divided.
        Hustle, little one. Gasp out an eddy
of steam. Now loose, you'll still make us wary
        about fever, oxygen valves.
An object in flight can oscillate itself
        to destruction, we know. But
this severing is necessary.
        This schism is sweet.

GODBABY

We say "He" without a name
       to speak of you,
hear our own sounds
       echoed back from far away
in the monitor's shush and fuzz.

At night, I hear you calling,
       but it's just a dog's whine outside,
a wheeze in my own breathing.
       Awake, you hold our hands
in your fat palms, then tug them

to your mouth, all tongue
       and palate, zest and tang.
In squall and agitation,
       you are unreadable,
vehicle too distant to send

clear telemetry. Rapturous
       in exhaustion, we
bow and circumambulate,
       we struggle to know
what you're thinking.

THIS IS MY BODY

I must admit: sometimes it
        disgusts me, night-lit
piranha jawing at my breast,
        the sensation of knotting
flesh just before he gets
        what he needs: water

to slake thirst, cream to fatten up.
        He gulps and grunts,
as he did in his first few
        minutes. Babies, born with
collapsed lungs, inflate them
        through their first breath.

Plucked from an incision, he struggled—
        blew a hole through one
small lung sac, alveolus, sent air
        into his chest. They wheeled
him away to the NICU, and a nurse
        shampooed his sticky hair,

gave him a bottle: plastic ease.
        Not until twelve hours later
did I get to hold him, trailing wires
        like a radio under repair. We
persevered: lactation consultant,
        pumping routine, four a.m.

in a secondhand rocking chair. Little
        dude, I give you my body,
fat and fluid retaining; my blood,
        altered, which will carry
your own cells, microchimeras,
        till they lodge in my organs.

I give you sugars and proteins, and,
        in minor doses, paint thinners,
rocket fuel, pesticides, flame
        retardants. I cannot help
but feed you the world as it is, even
        what I would rather not share.

APPROPRIATE CARE

The backyard fawn is, of course,
doe-eyed,
something between a baby
and youth. I'd
forgotten they might have
white spots
to blend in with grasses,
tree knots,
sun-flecked ground. If I moved
closer, she'd
smell like nothing,
ghost weed,
snow-in-summer. White-flecked
loner. Her
mother, odor-heavy, has left.
The fawn won't stir
till she returns. A friend who found
twin newborn deer
was told to leave them be unless
the mother disappeared
for a whole day. All this one needs
is oak shade.
My own baby stood there
yesterday, played
with a water table,
soaked his shirt
with ladle and cup. Even under my watchful
eye, he hurt
his lip when he stumbled.
At his daycare
the toddlers wobble and caper, testing
their balance on bare

feet. What do they do
in the interlude,
when parents don't observe?
Joyful or subdued
at play, perhaps, depending on the day,
a slight sadness
swelling in their torsos.
They're practiced
at waiting, knowing the door's
each creak
might be *she* returning,
her unique
footfall and smell. *Soon, any minute:*
the thought thumps
in hearts the size of golden
retrievers', as they jump
from a small step,
skin a knee,
burrow to sleep on their nap mats,
someone's sweet pea,
darling, dear.
Today, my fair-haired
boy, spoon-clutcher, *ooh*-er,
is not scared
of the ruminant under our tree.
He woofs,
the only animal sound he knows.
Her hoofs
are splayed to one side.
Seemingly complaisant,
she stares with her thin triangle face,
ears perked, patient—
or wary. At twilight, she'll join her
mother and
sister, find another yard, park,

grassland.
My son and I wave goodbye,
leave the window,
giving her privacy in this leafy
suburban limbo,
a good-enough way station
with strangers
watching over, able to help
look out for danger.

A SMACK OF JELLYFISH

In the children's zoo: an orb
    occupied by jellyfish, glass
at child's height, a light
    changing color perpetually,
the not-really-fish (medusae) themselves
    just transparent tissue
taking on the tangerine and lime hues.
    One floats more idly than

the rest, drawn by an imitation of
    current—artificially generated
or the others' wakes—mostly
    resting on the bottom, clearly
dead. Like the lattice of a pie-topper
    rolled out from dough and lifted over
apples or berries. When triggered, the tentacles'
    nematocysts pierce the skin

with venom, the plaque says,
    can bring on anaphylaxis.
When we saw a rash on our son's lip
    after peanut puffs, I held
his arms down while they scratched
    his back with allergens,
when they drew his blood into a
    syringe. If need be, I would

stab him with a needle to kick-start
    his heart, relax constricted
airways. To be fair, these bell-shaped
    gelatinous invertebrates
produce a collagen that might suppress

arthritis. You can scrape the stingers
off with a credit card, apply hydrocortisone,
        be fine. They use a form of

jet propulsion to move, together can be
        called a *bloom* or *smack* or *swarm*.
Mostly water, when they wash up on shore,
        they start to evaporate. Soft fossils
in sediment, they're preserved in Utah's
        ancient seabeds. A swarm at a nuclear
power plant's water intake shut it down.
        They'll likely outlive us as a species.

DOMESTIC CONCERNS

One man wrests a flag
from another, the two-ply
polyester whipping violently,
just one more splotch

in a riot of color—matched
hats, posters in every hue,
kinetic mosaic. They chant,
agitate. I cannot stand with them.

The work of civilization
is also laundry. Someone
has to sort clean socks
into pairs, fold them into

a symbol of union. Perhaps
she can read about the rallies while
she waits for the dryer to sing
its little hymn of conclusion.

TRY STAYING HOME

If you think going to the Moon is hard,
try staying home.

—Barbara Cernan, wife of astronaut Gene Cernan

WALLY FUNK (1962)

A pool the exact temperature of her body.
Her head covered in a plastic bag, her ears with headphones.
Nothing to hear but
the lockstep of breath.
Nothing to see but
the mirages a visual cortex
draws out of darkness.
You can't feel water
when you're immersed in it.
Decades later they'll weigh astronauts down
so they can stay forty feet below,
near the Shuttle mock-up, *neutral buoyancy*.
Floating on the surface, face down,
the aviator stays in the pool longer
than any other test subject.
They have to tell her to get out.
This is the closest she'll get to space for now:
adrift and tethered in a facsimile of flight.

VALENTINA PONOMARYOVA
(VALENTINA TERESHKOVA'S LAUNCH, 1963)

Valentina's colleague Valentina is vaulted into space
by an intercontinental ballistic missile.
Cosmonaut-in-training, Ponomaryova only watches,
her earthbound tailbone aching from
a hard wheat-field landing. She doesn't know
yet about the cracks in her spine from parachute training.

She doesn't know (but suspects)
she came in second because Khrushchev
liked Tereshkova's blonde Jackie-Kennedy look.
The official line: the other Valentina
is the ideal proletarian heroine,
former textile factory worker.
"It was a terrible moment, when Tereshkova took off,
and we were left behind. They told us, 'Don't fret,
you'll all get the chance to go to space.'"
Ponomaryova banks on a circumlunar flight
(cancelled), an all-female mission (scuttled).
The next female cosmonaut won't launch until 1981.

PAT WHITE (1968, APOLLO 8 LAUNCH)

Twenty-three months ago her astronaut-husband died
in the char of a hatch-sealed capsule
pumped full of oxygen and lined
with loose wires. But Pat White
joins the other astronaut wives at Susan Borman's.
Susan dithers, fidgets, a vessel of worry.
Drinks and hors d'oeuvres in a midcentury home,
cigarettes in front of the black-and-white TV.
In herringbone skirt and cream-collared blouse,
dark circles under her eyes, coiffed blonde hair,
Pat watches Susan from across the room.
"Man is about to leave this planet
for the first time. Odds are against
a major systems failure, but
if one occurred, the men could
be lost," a reporter intones.

The rocket vents gases, fastened to its gantry.
Susan can't stop agitating her hands;
she closes her eyes in a kind of regret
when the countdown reaches zero.

The rocket rising is the proverbial
candle (*Let's light this…*), but inverted,
somehow always fitting in the square of the screen.

"It's beautiful," says Pat from
the back row of the gathered.
We see her mouth move but can't
hear her over the thundering engines.
Frank Borman and his crew will be the first
humans to flee the grip of Earth's gravity.
Fifteen years later, days before
an astronaut-wives' reunion,
Pat will choose to flee herself,
sawing off a lock of her hair
for Thanatos, holder of an inverted torch,
so he'll approve her passage past life.

RALPH ABERNATHY (JULY 1969)

> *They must have been a sight: around 150 Americans,*
> *mostly black mothers and their children,*
> *walking with two mule-drawn wagons*
> *through light mist and rolling thunder.*

Ralph leads the Poor People's Campaign
across fields near Cape Canaveral.
85 degrees and humid.
It *is* quite a sight, mules
with a backdrop of palm trees
and the thirty-six-story,
red-white-and-blue Saturn V rocket
ready to carry the Apollo 11 crew
to the Moon tomorrow.
"Rockets or rickets?" one sign asks.

"If it were possible for us

not to push that button tomorrow morning
and solve the problems you are talking about,
we would not push that button,"
the NASA administrator comes over to tell Ralph.
(There is, of course, more than one button,
and most of the "buttons" are switches.)
He offers tickets to the viewing stands:
"I want you to hitch your wagon to our rocket."

The next morning, the arrival of the wave of sound
from the seething engines three miles away
throbs in Ralph's torso, a formidable leviathan:
*You are but a mist that appears for a little while
and then vanishes.*
This is holy ground, he thinks. It can be more holy.

KRISTIN FISHER (NOVEMBER 1984)

Astro-tot Kristin is startled as her grandmother shrieks.
Just fourteen months old, she doesn't understand
that the light-blue jumpsuit she's wearing
is official NASA fabric, the bright nonstar
striding across the Houston night sky
is a Shuttle holding her mother, 180 miles up.
She knows her father is holding *her,* that it's dark,
that the lake is sloshing under their dock.

Her mother, Anna, first mom in space,
has zipped herself into a sleeping pack
hanging from the wall. She doesn't
know what to do with her head
without a pillow. She still feels addled
from the vestibular weirdness of microgravity.
Tomorrow she'll frisbee-toss a satellite into space
using a robotic arm.

"How does operating the arm make you
a better mother?" a reporter asked before the flight.
"Oh, I don't think it did," she replied.

Kristin will write about her grandmother's
screaming—that unsettling sound—
her mother's celestial gallivanting,
as her first memory. "Well, that's really nice,
Kristin," the teacher will say, "but
you're supposed to tell a true memory."

KAREN NYBERG (MAY 2020)

The fiftieth woman in space is now earthbound,
in her favorite blue paisley handkerchief dress,
waving at her husband. She can't pass the yellow line
painted on the ground. They've quarantined together,
but still COVID-19, still flight protocols. He looks
like a twenty-fifth-century astronaut,
slick white flight suit, all slant and angle,
first NASA commander of a commercial flight vehicle.

Seven years since Karen last felt weightless,
one of only two women in space
on the fiftieth anniversary of Tereshkova's flight.
"It has raised the question, among some,
of why a mother left a toddler at home
to follow a dream into space,"
the local paper asked then, the same
as "some" did of Anna Fisher.
"How is that different from any woman
or man that has a career and has children?"
her husband, Doug, retorted.

It's 85 and muggy. Karen thinks of the chill

of the underwater habitat from years ago,
how she balanced in a moonsuit on the ocean floor,
metal frame strapped to her back mimicking
lunar gravity one day, Martian another.
Karen watches her husband leave twice,
first in the newfangled electric car with gull-wing doors,
then in an explosion of kerosene and liquid oxygen.
This weekend, city centers are filling
with people protesting the death of a Black man
under the knee of a white cop.
"If the space community wants to unite people,
then it must make people feel like they are part of space,"
the paper says, "and that means being conscious
of where people's lives are on the ground."

ROTATION

There is a resolute black seat belt.
      The thin aluminum rail
clinks to a close. It's just the right
      grip for a pair of anxious hands.
We swing up in the wheel, your first
      such ride, and I feel what you
must: the vestibular system of
      the earthbound body chirping

Something is very wrong, the stomach
      floating more loosely, giddy,
in the fluid-filled torso, the mind correcting.
      And despite your fear of slides,
of swings, of bounce houses
      in their earnest garishness, you revel.
The view holds steady briefly
      as we rock in stillness,

fairgrounds churning with
      the Friday-afternoon crowd,
cornfields patterning themselves
      as they do in June.
Oh, small person with all the
      tendencies I didn't want you
to inherit—sensitivity to noise
      and motion, weak lungs—

disciple of caution, I want you
      to be able to hold two opposing
truths about yourself consonant,
      the dread and the rapture.
The whirling we do for fun

exhilarates, is an imitation
of the ones we can't feel:
        our entire solar system

hurtling on its orbit around
        the galaxy, our movement
around and away from each other,
        me dropping you off at school,
returning in a circuit later that day.
        Your feigned or real protests
at the separation, your squeal
        of welcome when it ends.

BELATED VALENTINE WITH GEOLOGY AND PHYSICS

Love you like bedrock, our city's
        limestone & shale alternating,
born from prehistoric shallow seas
        & deltas, city where I met you, where
on good days synovial fluid with
        enough pressure

keeps my arthritic joints from
        aching. Love you like
docking latches, pneumatic system
        powered by nitrogen, holding
space modules together; like the deep
        dark vacuum outside

atmosphere, encompassing, the sheer
        cliffs of our geography,
late evidence of the glacier
        that pushed debris ahead of it
as it advanced, Paleozoic disaster
        that now affords invigorating
river views. Love you for

the myths you counter when
        we watch action movies:
an electromagnetic pulse would not
        turn off a city's lights.
A bullet cannot explode a gas tank.
        Love you like gravitational

waves, a distant catastrophe rippling our
        planet but all the diurnal

fiddle-faddle continuing: intermittent
    Weedwacker, honey too viscous
to cook with, child chortling in
    the other room as we share
the minutiae of the past few hours.

PUBLIC INTIMACIES

My mother never taught me
    to hover over the
public bathroom toilet,

    to avoid the heat
on the seat from another's
    skin. No matter

the cacophony of flushes
    and chatter around
the stall, the scents

    of other bodies,
we are essentially alone there.
    Just so, it's acceptable

to disrobe in
    the doctor's office,
don a paper gown,

    as routine as taking off
a belt in an airport
    security line. I admit I got

accustomed to
    covering my nakedness
with a sheet, shifting into

    the stirrups, letting
the fertility specialist use
    a wand to see

if my follicles were
          ripe for ovulation,
med students watching

          the monitor
to see which orbs
          were worth measuring.

I've omitted those
          details from my
previous accounts,

          resisted telling
even the closest
          of friends or family.

And in the surgical room
          for a C-section,
I begged my husband

          not to look at my
insides, tawdry entrails.
          There are places we can

bare ourselves
          and stay hidden, keep
the secrets of our

          bodies and how we feel
they've failed us. There
          are places teeming

with people where
          each of us is exposed,
but only for the sock-

footed walk
through the whirring
TSA scanner,

only for as long as
it takes
to suit up again.

SECONDARY INFERTILITY

an inability to conceive after a previous successful pregnancy

As if an astronaut had walked
       on the moon
after long preparations and delays,
       had pressed her boot into

the gritty surface of the Sea
       of Fertility, completed
every errand asked of her,
       even as her fingertips

bled in the pressurized gloves, as
       a pinkie nail
fell off, as she urinated
       into a Maximum Absorbency

Garment, and felt she was animal
       or child again,
had walked till her hips hurt,
       her suit soiled

by the dust that smelled like char,
       but she had done it,
no matter the cost, she had
       her new world, lunar body,

dark heaven, *she* bent to pick up
       an igneous rock
with the sheen of the frangible,
       a godsend that made

her exclaim into the muffle
        of her helmet,
"I think we found what we
        came for"—

but then on a second attempt
        years later,
this time to the moon's far side,
        the capsule leaking

fuel, malfunctioning, tumbling
        matryoshka doll, so she can see
the Icarus crater as they pass,
        knows the next mission

will descend, others will bound in joy
        as they possess the fields
with presence, a world lost to her,
        knows some will say,

"But you've already been—surely
        that's enough?"
"It's not the same moon," she'll
        want to say,

and she would slip into an alternate
        universe if she could,
the one where she was
        the first human to hold

a particular piece of the lunar surface
        again, each rock
unlike the last, revealing
        different primordial mysteries,

galactic cargo weighting down
         her elbow,
would prefer a reality in which
         she succeeded twice,

but this isn't science fiction.

LAVA TUBES ON THE MOON

Your voice saying *miscarriage* because I could not speak it into being
when the nurse asked why I was having surgery. You were my windbreak,
though you'd break down while you waited and I slept through the worst
of the loss. I hadn't realized
        you might grieve too
because it was happening inside *my* body, failed haven, genetic code
breaking down in the dark. Our first
        permanent dwelling on the moon
will likely be lava tubes, tunnels where lunar volcanoes' flow burned through
rock. O eerie
        cylinders, evidence of what's
died out, protect us from solar radiation. You *are a church,* you *are a sanctuary,*
the priest said online when churches closed their doors against a plague
this spring. But
        lava tubes on the moon have
skylights where magma bubbled up, clerestory windows we'd need to cover
to keep charged particles from changing our cells. I suspect we've never
seen extraterrestrials
        because they know a body
adapted to a particular place can't survive outside its biosphere for long.
Let's stay home in sweatpants and stuff our faces with spinach dip. Let's
say one more prayer from our religion for comfort; a conception is
        one of its central mysteries,
though it's one we don't seem to master well. Left out of the miracle
this time, we'll shore up the walls of the basement instead, our storm
shelter with
        a crack in the wall, with
only a lackluster glow from glass-block windows, radiation refracted
from a far-flung flaring star.

SOLITARY ROCKY CELESTIAL BODY

Asteroid half the size of a giraffe strikes Earth off the coast of Iceland...
—*Daily Mail* headline, March 14, 2022

An asteroid half the size of a giraffe
flies over Greenland's glaciers. Before
it detonates into a celestial fireball,
the tufts at the ends of its horns
toss like wind-borne dandelion fluff
in the breeze of atmosphere's resistance.
It feels its outer crust start to fuse
from the heat. The shavings of frost
on the tips of its russet mane
are starting to dissolve. It's dreaming
of grabbing acacia leaves with
its prehensile tongue in summer heat
as it soars over the gurgling volcanoes
of Iceland, toward its end above
the Norwegian Sea. It's mostly neck,
being only half a giraffe. Its rock is flecked
with metal from the collision that sent it
spinning our way. Oh leopard-print camel,
minor planet out of place, you flash like
the glint in an eye as a joke is told.
Don't tell us about being lonely. We know
what it's like not to find galactic companions.

POINT OF DEPARTURE

Forty-five miles per hour on the viaduct, early afternoon rush over train
yards where newly uncoupled freight cars ride slowly down a slope to
storage, I watched a car's hood, detached, rise up as if pulled by a string.
The sedan slowed at first, then sped away from the fifteen square feet of
steel on the road—

> Little speck, I forgot to sew you into my
> pocket. I swear we looked and looked and
> saw nothing where there should have been
> Something-You, flat layer of cells that
> lacked the code to build yourself a protective
> bubble. Invisible on the eerie gray crescent of
> the ultrasound, you peeled away at some
> point, lighter than a contact lens. I can think
> that but not say it without sorrow—

and because of how the road splits after the viaduct, lanes
curving away from each other, then crossing, I saw the
hoodless car drive past, front end mangled from a wreck,
impotent rope—former hood-lasher—dangling under the
bumper, the guts of the engines and hoses exposed, no way
to color that damage in gilded language or stay silent.

MOM IN SPACE

In space, to *move* is to *translate,*

as in   she carried a subaqueous nocturnal
        mammal in a bespoke pouch,
        translated it over maria—
        molten rock solidified
        over centuries—to the
        designated landing site,
        fired the descent engine,
        till the contact light blazed.

as in   she translated across the dining module
        to the high chair to turn the wide-eyed,
        open-mouthed child over
        and hit his back repeatedly
        between the shoulder blades
        until a piece of chicken
        just the size of a windpipe
        translated out onto the floor.

as in   she stared at the orange bottle,
        tried to translate the name
        of this month's medication into sense,
        move the complicated nomenclature
        to something her mouth could pronounce,
        its chalky discs ready to trick
        her pituitary, make the eggs
        inside her develop, fertile,
        moons that wax gibbous
        rather than leave a dark cyst
        in lieu of light.

as in   her body translated to the heavens,
        the equigravisphere, hanging
        between her two worlds, the child
        who was forged and welded
        into being, and the other just stardust
        and antineutrinos; she's been tranquil
        in the silence of the theoretical one—
        it knows how to soothe her in its
        neverness—but finally she's ready
        to get pulled into the calamity,
        slurry, gristle of reality, its forceful
        gravity, its robust communications
        array. She fires a booster on her jetpack,
        lets the planet's liquid iron core
        translate her into orbit once again.

VENUS

My daughter-never-born is throwing snow.
　　　She's dropping crystals
from clouds of sulfuric acid.
　　　They glisten like knives, swirl
in the solar winds. Each flake hovers

　　　over the ground before disappearing
into vapor. She smirks at her trickery,
　　　conjuring something
that changes form so quickly.
　　　The volcanic plains

are dry, oceans long gone.
　　　Water's hydrogen untangled
itself from oxygen, was sucked
　　　into space. A planet
needs a magnetic field to support life.

　　　A daughter needs an atmosphere
cool enough to breathe, not one
　　　hot enough to melt lead. A daughter
needs to move from mirage
　　　to materiality to be named.

THE YOUTUBE GAMERS MY SON WATCHES YELL CONSTANTLY TO DEMONSTRATE EXCITEMENT

They ululate. *Oh bro, oh bro, oh bro!* They emote.
They brandish their pickaxes
and mine ore, craft iron helmets for defense
against zombies, talking the entire time.
Oh-my-gosh, what-the-flip! They band together
to explore a village, eager, raucous. My son
watches alone, his elbow affixed to mine,
because everything is virtual,
because he can't play with other kids
unless it's outside, unless they're masked.
When he plays the game on his tablet,
he gets to pick what his face looks like.
He builds an underground fortress, then
wrecks it with TNT. Unable to produce
sibling playmates, I could blame
myself for his solitude. Oh parent friends,
I can't share your exasperation at the bulk
of double strollers. I've got nothing to say
about sibling rivalry. The evidence of
your ever-expanding families sometimes
galls me. I'm jealous of your successful
spontaneous pregnancies in your forties.
Defective reproducer, I tell my singleton
to turn the volume down
when the latest gamer shrieks.
He huddles silently on the couch
until his dad joins him and they enter
the same world on their tablets, a boy's voice
calling out like his idols—*Hey, dude,*
come and see this! You won't believe it!—
left foot crossed over his dad's legs
as if to anchor him there as long as possible.

SUPERMOMMY

Wears a cape made from a child's beloved blanket when asked.

Wears a corset after a C-section to feel like her insides will stay in.

Doesn't flinch at the crash of ice-fall from the eaves.

Marvels at the orderly miracle of morning drivers actually slowing to 20 mph in front of the middle school as required.

Knows that the word *shuttle* carries with it the bobbin traveling from one side of the loom to the other, and also harpoon, dart, missile: swiftness, lethality.

Once watched a robin peck and tear at a worm until it was in two pieces, and then a second robin landed, ready for the shared meal.

Brings her children squares flavored like cheese, bears that taste of graham flour, toast with the crust cut off, various seeds and beans and nuts.

Figured it was a lie that we conducted nuclear tests in outer space until she read about Starfish Prime.

Doesn't tell her children about Starfish Prime or the rest of Operation Fishbowl. Or about why they have to be quiet during lockdown drills. Or about the C-4 wedged in her genetic code, predisposition for spondyloarthritis, that she hopes they don't carry too.

Feels guilty that she's not preparing them for the rigors and pungency of corporeal existence because she *hasn't* told them these things.

Slows the car as she approaches a traffic armadillo flashing her speed for all the suburban audience to see.

Displays a picture of her children prominently on her desk at work, which is part of the formula for work-life balance. That and the right shoes and quick-prep meals.

Doesn't really like the word *mommy,* wishes she were Supermom or Superwoman or just Super, nonessentialized.

During any shut-eye, flies above her childhood habitat—crabapple tree, cranny behind the pine, frozen-custard stand, highway overpasses and interchanges—there and not there, trying to get back to something she doesn't understand.

Pretends she's not Super so as not to embarrass the other parents at afternoon pickup: wears the required athletic leggings and minimal makeup, just a soupçon of eyeliner; lets her son chatter as he tries and fails to buckle his seat belt, holding up the entire line of vehicles, until she unbuckles, runs around the car, and buckles him in herself, despite his vehement and shrill protests.

Knows that Hans Mark, a NASA center director, thought in the '80s that the development of Shuttle technology meant "even poets" could go into space, "then share the experience with everyone." Turns her cape into an orange pressure suit, plugs into the O_2 line and the communications cap, packs a life raft in her backpack.

Suspects that those with large families think she doesn't have enough children, and others think she has too many, shouldn't have had any at all, the climate is cratering, the earth is feverish.

Prefers the third person, the distance it engenders, the way it makes the quotidian sound like a myth, a cautionary tale, a hagiography. How in such fiction she can have as many children as she wants, can brag, blue-ribbon paragon, plucky.

Sometimes wants to visit Point Nemo, where space agencies send orbital junk, all those boosters and satellites and failed space stations rusting in the nutrient-poor water, just crabs and bacteria clustered around the deep volcanic vents, no fish, the South Pacific Gyre keeping organic matter and cool water away, no humans for more than a thousand miles; wants to fly there with her animal-print cape with the nubby gray side, spend some time alone in the quiet.

UNREMARKABLE

My deepest sadnesses are completely ordinary.
　　　Not the predicament of roundworms

　　　as the shuttle Columbia, making its way homeward,
is eaten through by heated plasma, leaving their thermos

falling solo through the stratosphere. No word
　　　can capture that experience, but

　　　so many lose a pregnancy that there's a name
for their children born later: rainbow babies.

The phrase harnesses the mythology of a watery disaster,
　　　a promise of future safety.

　　　I kept thinking my sorrow was something special,
but it was extraordinarily common.

The star-scar in my navel where they sewed me closed
　　　once they knew my pelvic girdle was free of adhesions.

　　　The sudden arrival back in the hospital bathroom
any time I used the same liquid soap

that made my hands smell like cold cream.
　　　A secret I kept coiled under my tongue

　　　as if it were a pill that would dissolve and render me
gravid. I was Saint Anne, patron of both the pregnant

　　　and the childless, stilled in a silver charm bracelet.
But so were those putting ribbons on their profile pictures

in October, light pink and baby blue. Do we really
          need another poem about this?

          The full Worm Moon in March obscured
by cloud cover is just another Mylar sphere

held up by a noble gas, not a fertility symbol. (After all,
          the roundworms survived. After all,

          some might say, *You've got a child at home;*
you were successful once.)

FILLING IN THE POND

Fish in the net whirr
      like an orange fan
at full speed, until they're at ease
      in the silty box of water.

We pump the backyard pond
      onto the lawn, cavity destined
to be a garden, and ankle-deep in
      the three inches of muck that remain,

he scoops out whatever has a heartbeat. The babies
      are silver, hard to sift from decaying leaves
and the string algae that clumps like green hair. Sure,
      we'd prefer to be more than three,

to multiply and be fruitful again, but some couples
      have no such luck, have instead
extra medication to inject, a calendar divided
      into two-week spans, the income to order

fill dirt for a former pond. The tiny silver fish
      will grow golden in another backyard.
It pours rain, a torrent, as we load them
      in the buyer's hatchback. The fish—

comets, fantails—used to gather, amazed,
      at the surface freckled by raindrops,
opening their mouths in slow O's.
      The UV filter we installed

for the pump, the lookout we kept
      for hungry raccoons: at some point
you have to call it quits.
      You have to decide to stop.

A white man in his seventies stands on a windy Florida launchpad talking to a journalist. He wears a checked short-sleeved shirt with a collar, and large oval glasses with a double bridge. He looks like my grandfather. You'd recognize his wide, toothy smile. Picture it behind an astronaut-in-training's helmet or in an open convertible in a ticker-tape parade. "It felt like a train on a bad railroad track," he says of his rocket to the Moon.

The journalist also interviews him indoors. It's 2005. The astronaut wears a smart corduroy suit jacket, like the men at my grandfather's country club.

"You said once to a reporter, 'How long must it take before I cease to be known as a spaceman?' Why'd you make that comment?" the journalist asks.

"I guess we all like to be recognized not for one piece of fireworks but for the ledger of our daily work," Neil says. His gray hair, otherwise carefully arranged, sticks out from behind one ear. "I wasn't chosen to be first. I was just chosen to command that flight. Circumstance put me in that particular role."

○   ●

When I say "my grandfather," I think I mean both of them, in their early nineties and sequestered during the pandemic in separate rooms at the same retirement community. One of my grandmothers passed away last year. The other is gone in a different way, living in a memory-care center.

My grandfathers were both born within a year of Neil. One of them flew a reconnaissance plane over the demilitarized zone after the Korean War, just a few years after Neil made bombing runs from an aircraft carrier there.

The other was a senior buyer for McDonnell Douglas for the space program. He oversaw a team of eight for the Gemini project "who bought all of the equipment for the capsule," he said, including the switches that helped Neil save himself and Dave Scott.

Because of my grandfathers, I used to think all men of that generation were take-charge, get-things-done, mostly stoic bootstrappers who liked to play golf.

○　　　●

Neil, counterpart for my grandfathers—but I too feel a kinship to him, feel like I recognize something in those blue twentieth-century eyes, the first to see a lunar field. I don't understand it entirely, but I've discovered:

Neil Armstrong was an early and ardent reader. He was born on August 5. He taught at the University of Cincinnati in the '70s.

I too: early and ardent reader. Born on August 6 (forty-nine years after Neil). Taught at the University of Cincinnati in the 2010s on a graduate assistantship while I worked on my doctorate.

○　　　●

And I miss space viscerally when I think about it, stomach tightening when welding fumes from our furnace upgrade fill the house, the scent in airlocks after a spacewalk. As if I've been there—not just in a cosmic sense, the cliché (and truth) that all our molecules are derived from ancient exploding stars. I feel forlorn when astronauts in films touch down on the ground.

But I get motion sickness on a long car or plane ride. I get dizzy even on the merry-go-round when my son, solitary child on the playground, wants to spin me. I've never been farther up than a commercial airflight. I have spondyloarthritis. I don't think anyone would let me board even the "vomit comet" parabolic flights where they can feign weightlessness, manufacture the sense that you've slipped loose from gravity.

○　　　●

Neil Armstrong knew something was wrong with his health on August 6, 2012, a day after his eighty-second birthday, the day of my thirty-third. He had reflux. He went in for a cardiac stress test and had a quadruple bypass the next day. During his recovery, a nurse pulled out a pacemaker wire that had been in place for the surgery—but not skillfully; Neil started bleeding into his heart.

When he died in Cincinnati on August 25, I would have been fifteen miles south of that hospital, except that I was on my way home from a writers' conference in Vermont, either in an airplane or an airport. "Terminal F in the Philly airport is gross," I wrote on social media. The next day I woke up with a cold.

○　●

My joints hurt if the barometric pressure falls more than three-tenths of a degree, my synovial fluid more susceptible to change.

Spacesuits are pressurized to help the lungs inflate and to keep any exposed bodily liquid from boiling, then evaporating in vacuum—but only to about a third of the pressure we experience at sea level, so that astronauts can still move their knuckles, bend their knees. In space, even with the joint-easing reduction of gravity, I would ache, stiff as a store mannequin who needs another's hand to move her, just one joint covered in Neoprene-coated nylon and white Teflon, move it just a little, then another.

○　●

The men who flew to the Moon were five times more likely to have died from heart disease than those who stayed earthbound. Outside Earth's magnetosphere, they soaked up solar particles, changing the cells that lined their blood vessels.

○　●

Fifty years after Neil stood in the solar particles of a lunar morning, our local museum—where he'd been a board member—

exhibited the Apollo 11 command module, an eleven-foot-tall relic of a Cold War crusade. Across the room were his handwritten edits on a museum-gala speech he gave in 1993: "It is not easy to predict the next 175 years—but we just might give you a preview. [...] It's probably true that some folks are indifferent to museums. They are not into dynosaurs and plants and ice ages. There are important problems of today—like the budget deficits and global warming."

Because I stood marveling at the displays too long, my hip joints ached as my husband and I walked to the car to head home to our son and his babysitter, and I felt residual pain for several days after. That was October 2019. I was still a few weeks away from meeting with my second-opinion rheumatologist, the one who started me on the right meds.

Four months later, in February 2020, I sat on the Florida beach of a writing residency, reading about the Apollo program: Neil within a larger context, hundreds of thousands of people in private companies and at NASA working together to engineer a moon shot, and then another. And another. Until Gene Cernan looked one last time at the Taurus mountain ridge before he closed the hatch.

When I finished the book, I wanted to learn what happened next. In March 2020 I began the work of studying spaceflight, poring over books about Skylab, the shuttle program, Mir, the International Space Station, the year astronaut Scott Kelly spent in space. And while I did so, we all began to stay at home. A pandemic raged, my body hurt, but I could escape to space.

○　　　　●

There aren't very many still pictures of Neil Armstrong on the Moon. He was the one with the camera. Here he is reflected in Buzz Aldrin's visor. Here are his legs in shadow. Here's his back, from a distance.

The pictures I have of my son are, in descending order, in these categories: 1) my son alone, 2) my son and my husband, 3) selfies I took of me and my son, 4) shots of me holding my son.

I should clarify that my husband changed nearly every diaper in the first few months of my son's life, even if he wasn't quick with a camera shutter. I'd been on near-bedrest with pelvic muscle pain during the end of the pregnancy, and then my abdominal muscles were sliced into for a C-section. It took a while to get up. It hurt to hold even the weight of my baby if I was standing. And, swollen with hormones, I didn't really want my picture taken.

○　　　●

"You're going to have to write mommy poems now," a male classmate told a friend when he heard she was pregnant. I watched another guy's eyes glaze over as, in the midst of the work of pregnancy, I read from an essay about worrying my baby would die, about returning again and again to an online forum where one mom posted regularly about her late miscarriage in process.

Even as I wrote about the experience, I felt strange in a pregnant body, essentialized as woman, reduced to the biology of my reproductive organs, not always recognized as a holistic being with many facets: teacher, poet, citizen.

I guess we all like to be recognized not for one element of who we are but for the ledger of our daily work.

○　　　●

Neil was notoriously reticent, especially about his feelings. Few of his colleagues in the NASA years knew he'd had a daughter who died of childhood cancer before that. His first wife divorced him after thirty-eight years of marriage due to "years of emotional distance," according to a biography.

In the video, the television journalist asks Neil about the death of his two-year-old daughter, how he kept working. "I thought the best thing for me to do in that situation was to continue with my work, keep things as normal as I could, and try as hard as I could not to have it affect my ability to do useful things," he says, with a tone somehow of both regret and resolve.

In the week before Muffie's death, Neil was traveling for his job. Five days after her funeral, he was once again at work as a test pilot for a spaceplane that, boosted by a rocket, could make a hypersonic flight into the upper atmosphere and glide back to an airfield, a design that Shuttle planners (and Virgin Galactic) took into account years later.

And in 1968, after he nearly crashed in a spidery vehicle that helped the astronaut corps train for lunar landings—ejecting before it hit the ground—he went to his desk and did paperwork. "There was work to be done," he says jokingly when the journalist asks him about it.

○　　　●

I found both of my grandfathers intimidating. They were not the type to get down on the ground and play with a young girl, even if she was the first grandchild on both sides. When we gathered as a family, they watched sports—golf, Saint Louis Cardinals baseball or football—in their dens, one wood paneled with a tile floor, the other a basement walkout. I remember them as being upset or frustrated most of the time, but I think now that it was mostly the poorly performing Cardinals football team, which left the city in 1988.

I know other family members have wider experiences with these two men, saw their full range of emotions, not just their disappointment at a flubbed fourth down, their sorrow at their mothers' gravesides during the cemetery service.

○　　　●

On Gemini 8, Neil and Dave Scott were the first to rendezvous and dock with a target vehicle, in the counterintuitive system of orbital mechanics (faster is lower, slower is higher). But then they began to roll uncontrollably, a yaw thruster on their capsule misfiring.

Imagine tumbling more than 360 degrees in a second, the panels in front of you hazy and blurred. Don't pass out. Blow the squib valves on the other system meant to control your spacecraft, the one used only for reentry. You won't bounce off the atmosphere. You won't land in hostile territory. You will feel seasick as you wait for the navy frogmen to airlift you out of the Pacific.

○　　　●

My own disasters have been mostly of my body's making. My appendix went haywire and perforated. My ovaries failed to fire as they should for a healthy conception. My immune system is an assailant—first just creating antigens to dust and pollens, then attacking my thyroid, then going for my joints.

○　　　●

Only in the past year have I learned that we're closer to the sun in the winter. It's the 23-degree tilt of the planet that makes the sun's rays hotter in summer. Some geologists think a protoplanet struck the early Earth, spinning it into our current 24-hour day, tilting it at that livable axis, spewing debris into orbit more than 238,000 miles away, which circled and circled until it formed the orb of our Moon.

○　　　●

I realized my loss of joint flexibility wasn't just aging when my neck lost its curve, so I couldn't kiss my six-foot husband for longer than a peck without needing to straighten out again. If I hold his hand too long while we watch a movie, my knuckles get stiff. "Too long" is often just ten minutes.

So it's not just motion sensitivity and lower air pressure keeping me from a flight to space: sitting still for a launch would temporarily cement my hip joints; afterward, I wouldn't be able to stand up to more than a crouch at first. My elbows would be reluctant to unbend from their positions on the armrests. My tendons would shudder.

And my son is disturbed if I go into the next room, much less leave for two weeks. During that writing residency in Florida, my first since his birth (he was four), I felt guilty every day.

○   ●

I didn't write much when my son was a baby and toddler. If there was time, there wasn't enough synaptic energy. Plus, I felt like I didn't have anything to say. I wrote a few mommy poems.

But lately, I read about spaceflight. I compose poems about a mom in space. I've written more in a year than in the previous four years combined. Typing hurts my right hand, so I wear a wrist brace or a compression glove. I make sure to get up every half hour so my sacroiliac joint stays flexible.

For years, I felt like I wasn't doing the important work, as my son woke early from his nap, as he asked me to watch him drive a car down a ramp in exactly the same way more than twenty times in a row, as he leaned against me while we watched TV. I didn't think of work widely enough. I didn't think about how it involves one body supporting another.

○   ●

Admit it, Lisa. This essay—this work—is what it is because Neil reminds you of your grandfathers, because your forebears were more like him than the Black protesters in the '60s calling for the money spent on the space program to go to antipoverty programs.

This essay isn't about Ron McNair or Guion Bluford. It isn't about Mae Jemison. Admit, too, that the combination of ambition and humility he embodies is what you strive to project, the striving itself a kind of antihumility.

○　　●

This essay is what it is because in the first season of the pandemic, as I waited for an expensive medication to tame my overactive immune system, I watched the 2018 movie about Neil, *First Man*. It was like trying to understand a brother I'd been separated from at birth. I felt dizzy with the spin rate of the Gemini capsule. I could imagine myself into the spidery aluminum lunar-lander trainer. It's about to crash—can I eject on time? Will the interplay between my parachute and the wind carry me into the flaming wreckage?

Ryan Gosling, the twenty-first-century man in a costume and makeup, made of pixels assembled on a screen: I like to believe he captured the Neil who bought a farm just north of here after retiring from NASA, who'd walked the halls of the engineering building on the campus where I work. I like to think that he got that unassuming, charismatic reticence just right.

We all craft our selves every day, of course. I conceal my anxiety with foundation and bronzer, with an "I Need Space" shirt. I'm not here, my SI joint doesn't hurt, I'm just trying to figure out what the 1202 alarm code in the LEM means as we approach the gray dust of the Sea of Tranquility.

Reticence is a facial mask applied with clay so that the only expression you can make is tight-lipped, aloof, self-effacing.

Is this essay itself too reticent?

○　　●

"The one thing I regret was that my work required an enormous amount of my time, a lot of travel, and I didn't"—he holds his face still in a grimace for a microsecond—"get to spend the time I would have liked with my family as they were growing up," Neil admits to the journalist.

B-roll footage shows him walking around his childhood farm. It must be fall; the corn stalks are dried out and browning. "In the autumn of his life, he lives very much in the present," the journalist's voice-over explains, "refusing to let his famous deed define him. He's made a comfortable living serving on corporate boards."

In the final scene, two planes fly, one towing the other. A wire between the two falls away, and the sailplane, engineless, glides.

"It's the closest you can come to being a bird," Neil tells the journalist. He smiles (wide, toothy) with the joy of a teenager given his first flying lesson. He has seven more years left with his beloved second wife, his sailplane, his corporate boards, his golf course and country club in one of the toniest suburbs of Cincinnati, his paid speeches.

In his final such speech, the opening of a new telescope at an Arizona observatory, he will joke that he was just a technician for an experiment to help calculate how far away the Moon lies. "My job was to install the mirrors. We had to have some way of confirming the mileage for our expense account."

He placed the angled panel with more than a hundred mirrors where he was told to. He hauled boxes of rocks so they could be hoisted by Aldrin up into the ship. His heart rate spiked to 160 bpm in the final few minutes of packing, before he climbed the ladder to fly home to the work of the rest of his life.

SELF-PORTRAIT AS LASER INFEROMETER SPACE ANTENNA (LISA)

with language from lisa.nasa.gov

In space, LISA can avoid the noise of Earth
and access distant regions of the spectrum,
listening for gravitational waves with every

instrument in her three-bodied self.
She tends to remember the nitty-gritty
details of each of those bodies—from

which bread they like best to the last location
of the most beloved lovey. She'll marshal
the three spacecraft separated by millions

of miles, which fly in the Earth's wake
as it orbits the Sun. They'll all get
to the right place at the right time,

as long as she provides the right mix of fuel
(fruit snacks, apples, light beer, salsa)
and rest. She can conjure up waffles

when the bread's gone moldy.
This equilateral triangle of spacecraft
has three "arms" that extend to detect

ripples of violence from eons ago.
With her extremely long arms, LISA
can hold herself still. The digital thread

connecting them pulses with data,
coding a family out of three integers.
She requires the precision of picometers,

can note a shift in space-time less than
the diameter of a helium nucleus
over a million miles away. Just ask her

what that muscle twitch in the starboard
face of one spacecraft means. She's got
an ear adapted to hear the roar from

two stars merging as they pass too close
to a black hole, maybe even the whisper of
quantum fluctuations in the early universe.

LISA's in a customized package
optimized for spaceflight. Her lasers
must operate for generations

in the harsh environment of space,
the acidic dark of near-vacuum.
She'll push past the stiffness in her joints,

chilled in the disinterested deep-freeze.
She will ride the gravitational waves,
measure the level of imperfection

as the delicate gold instruments
in the safe cavity of her interior
free-fall. With her help, we'll

be able to detect ancient distortions
in the stretchy fabric of space-time
from disasters we won't ever witness.

AUTOIMMUNITY AND MICROGRAVITY

After a year outside Earth's protection, one returned astronaut's
skin rashed up
wherever it was touched, allergic to terra firma, the immune system
righting itself

by lashing out. Old viruses reactivate in space, T cells speaking less
clearly to their troops
without the drag of gravity. And then there's the radiation,
ten X-rays' worth per day,

photons flashing cosmically even through closed eyelids, streaking
across the retina,
personal starshow that can keep a human body from sleep. In the morning,
I wake up stiff,

sacroiliac joint and spinal column temporarily ossified like a med-school
skeleton. Sly
and cunning back pain, cytokines attacking my internal fittings.
One fateful tweak

in my sixth chromosome guiding an antigen on white blood cells
to misperform.
Some nights I dream my hips are so rigid I walk with an altered gait,
I climb stairs as if

wearing a concrete skirt. Spondyloarthritic, a mouthful of a word
meaning
when the immune system turns on the joints, it doesn't worry about
the havoc it creates.

When superheated pink plasma seeped through a hole in
the orbiter's wing,
after all, it was just air broken apart into ions, doing
what comes naturally,

not concerned about the disaster to come. Disaster, after all,
descending from
"ill-starred," my unlucky astronomy,
my antimatter parts.

A/STEROID

with a debt to Destiny O. Birdsong's "Auto-immune"

It's foolish to think that the word *asteroid*
without its initial *a* becomes *steroid,*

one descending from a Greek *starlike,*
the other a twentieth-century sterol + oid.

But I like to imagine my lab-created med
as an astral compound, my three-pill steroid

dose making my face as puffy as an astronaut's
in the fluid shift of microgravity. Corticosteroids

curtail inflammation, tame the berserk
immune system, aren't the anabolic steroids

bodybuilders sneak, though I'd love the sinew
and stamina they acquire. With my steroid,

I settle for joints that don't feel filled with lava,
accept jacked-up hunger, ghastly dreams. Steroids

are a compromise in a body set against itself.
Rocky celestial body or starfish, an asteroid

can't come to me in a bottle labeled *Lisa.*
Hallelujah for my holy/unholy steroid.

THE SHADE ON MERCURY (AILEY CRATER)

> From his roots as a slave, the American Negro—sometimes sorrowing, sometimes jubilant, but always hopeful—has created a legacy of music and dance which have touched, illuminated, and influenced the most remote preserves of world civilization. I and my dance theater celebrate this trembling beauty.
>
> —1964 program notes for Alvin Ailey's *Revelations*

No cash bar on your namesake crater, Alvin,
since it's cold enough on Mercury to freeze alcohol—
it'd be hard to find a more remote venue. In a taste
of home, to open the final movement of the dance,
women in gold A-line dresses wave wicker fans
in near-vacuum, generating no wind. They carry
four-legged stools, greet each other with elaborate
flapping of their fans. Charged particles, sodium
and oxygen kicked up by solar wind, hover
above them, waiting for something to spark,
though when the sun rises, they'll burn away.
The women turn their backs to us, place
their stools in unison on the chalky floor
of the crater, which looks like a shoeprint
from above, landslides eroding the walls.
All nine of them sit slowly, legs wide, somehow
pirouette without standing again. They partner
with men in black pants and gold vests, stand,
church congregation in step.

                          Now the sun, overdazzling, rises
                          (sky black with the lack of atmosphere),
                          ascending only partway before
                          it stops, slides backward, the planet's
                          speed around the star swifter
                          than its internal spin, the ground
                          hot enough to melt lead, the dancers

boogying to gospel music, *Head
got wet with the midnight dew. Morning
star was a witness too.*

The shade edges closer, the sun gone
below the horizon, but this blackness
is a relief, safe place, church haven,
the moving figures are birds, no, a parade.
They're never finished when you think
they are, just starting a new movement,
all *menace and funk. Sometimes sorrowful,
sometimes jubilant,* you called your art
in 1964, as the Texan president signed
the Civil Rights Act, as the bigots ironed
their robes. Still, *this* part isn't about trauma

and the sky is bright again, never blue,
the yellow dwarf close enough to dominate
this dance designed around your *blood
memories* of rural Texas in the '30s, revival
and revelry, even when they're kneeling
with their arms in crisp Vs, still,
that's not the end, the men fan themselves
in cordial parody, walk on their knees
toward the back of the crater
as the women clap and lift their faces
to the light, animating the vision
of *a Black man whose roots are in the sun
and dirt of the South,* as you called yourself,
remembered here on an isolated planet
the dance company has made its own, far
from the one that lacked full beauty,
that still lacks it. Instead, inhabit
this pitted surface whose craters chronicle
that period of late heavy bombardment,
when asteroids and failed planets scarred
those that go on spinning.

MAE & NICHELLE, IN SPACE & ON EARTH

Floating in microgravity—with the grace of a ballerina, in a baggy blue jumpsuit—Dr. Mae Jemison, the first Black woman in space, anesthetizes four female South African clawed frogs. She injects them with HCG to stimulate ovulation and leaves them in the privacy of a quiet tank to lay their eggs. She must first kill the males, then inject fluid from their testes onto the eggs—no romance here in space. Tadpole astronauts born four days later develop normally, the NASA scientists will conclude, with slightly smaller lungs.

At the porthole, Mae looks down three hundred kilometers at the southside of Chicago, where, as a girl, she played Barbies, took ballet, and watched *Star Trek* in the late '60s. She climbs into a lower-body negative-pressure apparatus, which pulls her blood back down toward her feet, a five-hour experiment that imitates the pull of Earth.

"Strong inference on subspace, Captain," Lieutenant Uhura says at her twenty-third-century comm panel. "The planet must be a natural radio source." And then it's the '70s, and actress Nichelle Nichols, in a blue jumpsuit and carefully teased hair, sits at the console of a bulky computer, waving a number two pencil. "The space shuttle is built to make regularly scheduled runs into space and back, just like a commercial airline," she tells us. Astronaut Alan Bean gives her a personal tour of Johnson Space Center, helps her into a lower-body pressure device to check her heart under stress. "The *Enterprise* was never like this," she quips.

Nichelle Nichols has a history with the stars: she studied at the Chicago Ballet Company, toured with Duke Ellington, appeared in a James Baldwin play in Los Angeles, was friends with Maya Angelou. She wanted to quit *Star Trek* after learning the network had been purposefully holding back her fan mail, but Martin Luther King Jr. asked her to stay. "For the first time, we are being seen the world over as we should be seen," he told her.

And a history with the astral, too: her brother Thomas fatally believed the dogma of Heaven's Gate, that he could evolve past humanity, ascend to a ship hidden in a comet's wake. She was there when the space shuttle prototype, Enterprise, rolled out to fanfare. At age 84, she flew into the lower atmosphere with a telescope built into a 747. An asteroid in the belt between Mars and Jupiter is named for her:

—because Nichelle changed the face of the astronaut corps. "The Shuttle will be taking scientists and engineers, men and women of all races, into space, just like the astronaut crew on the starship *Enterprise*. . . . This is your NASA," she tells "minorities and women alike." Soon, Sally Ride applies, and the first Black astronauts, and the first Asian American, and four of the astronauts later assigned to the 1986 *Challenger* flight. Then in 1985, as soon as she qualifies, a young physician and chemical engineer, Mae Jemison.

MAY 1993; "SECOND ACTS," *STAR TREK: THE NEXT GENERATION*

The junior transport technician in black-and-citrine uniform studies the readings on her touch-screen console. "Phase distortion is dropping. The next transport window opens in forty-two seconds." It's guest star Dr. Mae Jemison, her hair as close-cropped as it was in space. Most of the episode centers on a man having an argument with himself, doubled in a transporter malfunction. The faux stars outside the window do not move or twinkle, but atmospheric rivers eddy on the planet below. Nichelle Nichols, catalyst for the gig, waits offstage. Mae has morphed: from audience, to astronaut, to actress:

—to arrested. In February 1996, the first Black woman in space is pulled over in Nassau Bay, Texas, for an illegal turn. The officer tells her she's under arrest for a speeding ticket she thought she paid years ago. In frustration, she throws her keys to the ground. But the officer is already handcuffing her as she leans over to pick them up. He "grabs her left hand, knocking her wallet and paper out of it, twists her wrist and throws her arms up behind her back," as her lawyer will later describe it. She's forced down, grit against her cheek, then concrete coarse under her bare feet as he muscles her to the patrol car, the materials of earth keeping her grounded. She'll be held two hours until she posts bail. It's like the plot of a one-hour sci-fi show, if the police were aliens on an off-kilter planet—except that an investigation will clear the officer, and the plot seems almost like a cliché, repeated ad infinitum. If she were back on the show, they'd fire the interstellar engines, steer the ship far away, toward some more welcoming galaxy.

MAY 2018, MAE JEMISON ON *GOOD MORNING AMERICA*

"I want you to do something for me. I want you to go outside and look up.

Because you're looking into space and infinity. When you're up above the Earth's atmosphere, there's a little less light pollution, and so you see the stars more abundantly.

But remember, right now we're on a spaceship."

In a citrine jacket, bright pop of color in the darkness of the television studio, Mae looks into the hulking camera apparatus, speaking directly to the girl who asked, "What is it like to be looking at the universe, knowing it never ends?" When the next video autoplays, she's twenty-six years younger, floating in the brightly lit SpaceLab, tethered to a wall by a wire, another life-science experiment that will help future astronauts survive the damaging effects of space.

STAY-AT-HOME CHRONICLES

I miss space, when I'm not
          reading about it, the isolation
of the Station, closed circuit,
          water recirculator pulling H_2O
from exhalation and sweat,
          molecule to potable.

Here, lethargic yellow jackets
          keep showing up inside,
the females, pest control says,
          woken up early, searching out
the right spot for a nest. We're not
          sure how they get in.

One module of the Station
          infamously had a drilled
hole, atmosphere slowly leaking out
          to vacuum till they
noticed. Our fridge abruptly
          whirrs as the ice maker

pulls in a stream of water,
          hurtles a cold cube
into the dark freezer.
          I dream a psychopath
is preparing to kill repeatedly.
          We fashion a mask

from a T-shirt. My son
          calls it *the king virus,*
and I keep him away
          from the vespine interlopers.
He runs barefoot after
          my husband mows

the lawn, squeezes clippings
      in his fists,
hands and feet stained green,
      face flushed with
a temporary joy. On the Station,
      after they grew red

romaine leaves, they
      dressed some with balsamic
and olive oil and ate them,
      the clay soil that nourished
the greens ensconced safely in a Teflon-
      coated Kevlar pillow.

I put on a gold-plated visor
      when I talk to my son
so he sees only the reflection
      of the sun, not the worry
in my features; I've forgotten
      how to relax

my jaw; I dream of sleeping
      in a narrow crew cabin
for one, strapped into
      a sleeping bag, my arms
tucked in so they don't float,
      ghostly, above my head;

I wake in the living room all
      three of us inhabit, under
a pile of plush loveys my son
      has assembled, that
game of burial but
      comfort, once again.

SPACE PASTORAL

This is *Friendship 7*. I'll try to describe what I'm in here.
I am in a big mass of some very small particles, that are brilliantly
lit up like they're luminescent. I never saw anything like it.

—John Glenn

If the prairie is thermosphere, fireflies
are frost sloughing off a metal capsule
that streaked from Florida into orbit,
heated then chilled then heated in sunrise
and -set sped up. The snowflakes luminesce.
They star-shower. They fail to seek a mate,
bound to the speed of falling, orbital
mechanics. In another life I hiked
through them in dusk, beetles tessellating
the fields, extinct stars brighter in the lack
of atmosphere. I mooned over a flirt
light years away. Ugh, I carried a torch,
for goodness' sake. I longed for something
simpler, the plasma fireball, reentry.

SPACE FLORA AND FAUNA

> In the Space Station, "plastic particles are weightless,
> as is the air, so they mingle in every breath."
> —astronaut Scott Kelly

To swallow plastic must feel familiar,
        as close to home   as a habitable artificial
satellite can get, every surface

off-gassing that new-car smell
        even though parts   of its corpus
have been in orbit for decades.

To you astronauts, paragons
        of our species,   broken-down polymers
bobbing like dandelion spores

in the air are nothing. After all,
        we mammals are   used to micro-
beads blooming in estuarial soil,

chemicals making a river smell
        like licorice.   Compared to plastic
or bacteria, we're ephemeral.

I'm sure you've read the study
        in which *D. radiodurans*   cells
survived being blasted with

ultraviolent, gamma, and X-rays
        on the Station's hull: extremophile,
a parallel (flawed, perhaps) to

your own exploits, as you risk
        radiation exposure for   the sake
of science and personal adventure.

You would have clung to the asteroid
      whizzing across our   solar system,
just like the cyanobacteria on its pits,

gripping tight even as the rock-chunk crash-landed
      on our terrestrial sphere,   seeding life.
At some point two billion years ago

that blue-green algae began venting
      oxygen, ozone,   which thickened
and became atmosphere, durable layers

of which save us from "the Sun's
      molecule-hostile   ultraviolet photons."
Circumscribed, cotton-encompassed world

in which we intertwine, except for
      you chosen few who   ride a raptor
up to a tin can simulating the ventilation

of our planet. You've tried to explain
      to us earth dwellers how   each spacecraft
is its own quick-witted beast, breathing

and settling. One of you, describing
      the ride home through   the mesosphere,
said the newfangled capsule "doesn't

sound like a machine; it sounds like an animal,"
      thrusters puffing, thick air   shuddering
with the friction, brilliant pink plasma

juddering on the porthole. To leave
      the Station, you need to   ride inside
a mechanical horse through a windstorm,

threads of frost spiraling from its mane,
        the balmy interior starting   to sweat.
You won't be able to move your head.

The rest of your species will watch the horse's
        televised descent   into the oil-marred
Gulf, its sooty hooves thrashing in the surf.

BREAKING THE WHEEL

As a child, I lived
    on Saint Catherine Street,
        patron saint of unmarried girls

and knife sharpeners,
    spinsters and spinners.
        Strapped to a spiked wheel for torture

when she wouldn't
    consort with the emperor,
        she shattered it with her touch.

Impatient, the executioner
    took her head instead.
        At one end, Saint Catherine Street

becomes Greengrass. In the middle,
    we sledded down the front-yard hill,
        whooping with joy or terror.

The street dead-ends
    near Coldwater Creek
        with its concrete banks and nuclear secrets:

runoff from radioactive waste
    leached into its water
        decades ago. The kids who played

on its banks (my mother
    never let me) have
        salivary gland growths, thyroid tumors.

In one treatment, neutron therapy,
      the radiation takes away
            from what it gave.

In the room, a "vault,"
      photons bounce off a bit
            of beryllium, and the tumor's DNA

dances in the ray,
      cannot cope. The cell
            breaks, defeated wheel.

For years, the official word
      was: no link between
            their illness and the creek.

Now the state sifts the soil.
      Thorium lurks a few feet down.
            Don't breathe it in,

the researchers warn;
      no landscaping or tilling here.
            Use caution. We can clean this up.

Caravaggio's Catherine holds a sword,
      her dress sleeves white
            against the dark shadows of her skirts.

The wheel is broken behind her,
      two spokes with empty couplings.
            An unbroken halo curves

around her head, barely there,
      gold that might
            float away on the lightest exhalation.

MIDDEN

Manasota Key, Florida; Bridgeton, Missouri

She wants to show me the midden,
       rocky dune bulldozed
in the '50s to make way for the path
       that leads to the dock
at Lemon Bay. Just arrived,
       I want only a nap.

Later, I'll understand: It's one of a series
       of terraformed mounds,
some even keys off the mainland,
       the prehistoric indigenous Calusa
reworking dump sites—
       piling "debris of human

activity," animal bones, shells
       used for scraping food,
then tossed. Each piece ordinary
       in its own way,
till they repurposed it
       for contriving an island.

I come from a region
       that glaciers buffed
flat till they stopped and piled
       up moraines—
but not everyone needs
       a massive icy force

to push the land into
       what they require.
And where I grew up,

                    they spread Manhattan
Project nuclear waste
          atop the landfill,

barium sulfate from enriching
          uranium "mixed in
with soil as top cover."
          A subsurface fire near my
hometown has smoldered
          for more than a decade,

now about a thousand feet away
          from that Superfund site.
It smells like "rotten cabbage,"
          "like a house is on fire," should
burn itself out in the next five years,
          if it doesn't breach

the firebreak. They've added
          a cap—rock, clay, soil—to stifle
the stench, tracked the fire's spread
          by seeing where plastic bags
partially combusted are "gummy black."
          The midden, alkaline heap,

pH of the shells delaying
          decay, will at some point become
reef, when the bay and Gulf meet,
          the glaciers of our time
forsaking the poles and melting
          into sea.

"THE FUTURE ISN'T WHAT IT ONCE WAS"

—Neil Armstrong, 1993 speech at the Cincinnati Museum
of Natural History

Even Neil Armstrong talked
    about global warming,
in a gala lecture, his handwritten

    speech revisions
on display here, Apollo
    anniversary exhibit.

He said then
    that the predictions
were wrong, the science

    would turn, deep strata
of polar ice drills
    showing trapped gases,

tree rings in
    old-growth Chilean alerce
indicating the Industrial

    Revolution didn't
begin to doom us.
    He and other human bodies

may have warmed
    the surface of the moon
as much as six

    degrees Fahrenheit
with the dark dust
    they kicked up: regolith.

Nearly half a million
         people worked
for the U.S. space

         program. The rocket
that propelled
         those three as they left

our collective sphere
         burned twenty tons of fuel
per second. Aldrin's gold visor

         still reflects whatever's
in front of it—visitors
         with cameras. Their

survival kit for landing
         included a desalinator
for sea water,

         sunscreen, a machete.
Armstrong died
         from internal bleeding

in a suburban
         hospital, pacemaker
wires from bypass surgery

         pulled out wrong. That same
year, 97 percent
         of the Greenland ice sheet

showed signs of melt: a record.
         The exhibit's centerpiece
is the great capsule, ten

feet high, tanned
with earth tones from
    the heat of reentry,

blunt-end design
    in which the three
shuddered with the friction

    as they pierced the
atmosphere, part of
    the body once again.

ACQUIRING THE FIRE

I never felt I stole anybody's fire
(I merely carried it through the sky).
　　—Michael Collins, in *Carrying the Fire*

I.

Space smells like seared steaks, spent gunpowder, welding fumes—the aftermath
of fire, as dangling ions from hydrocarbons find oxygen in a vehicle's pressurized
interior. And there's a sweetness, an ester alcohol that flavors raspberries, smells
like rum, occurs naturally in ants and bee stingers. With no air molecules to carry
vibrations, there are no sound waves outside atmosphere. "The constant nuclear
conflagration of the Sun would be completely deafening if not for the emptiness
of space"—imagine the crack and sizzle, how it would impair any astronaut who
ventured alone outside a capsule's titanium shell.

II.

Gemini 9-A, June 1966
Tom Stafford and Gene Cernan

Stafford and Cernan couldn't rendezvous with their target, the upper stage
of a rocket designed to stand in for the lunar module still in production: its
protective clamshell shroud failed to jettison. Instead, the strobe-lighted, partially
opened docking adapter rotated slowly in orbit, "angry alligator," useless for the
experiment.

So Cernan donned his cream-colored nylon pressure suit with metallic pants and
climbed out the hatch, attached to an umbilical. With no handholds or footrests,
he spun. His stiff outfit had "the flexibility of a rusty suit of armor." He finally
lurched to the bulky backpack stored on the rear of the capsule, a jetpack powered
by hydrogen peroxide, his heartrate flaring to 155 beats per minute. He fogged
his faceplate and couldn't see. He called it quits, left the experimental unit where
it was, pulled himself back hand over hand on the tether. Stafford had to grab his
leg to get him back into the capsule: he couldn't bend with the suit pressurized.

After reentry, on the deck of the USS *Wasp*, he poured sweat out of his boots. He'd lost ten pounds on the walk. Three years later, Neil Armstrong would have a water-cooling system in his suit, an antifogging visor. What one team learned, they all did.

III.

Saint Louis, February 1966
Deaths of Elliot See and Charlie Bassett

Stafford and Cernan, ensconced in their supersonic T-38 twinjet, realized they couldn't land and climbed up for a fly-around, into the low ceiling of cloud and snow flurries. The backups for Gemini 9, they were traveling with the prime crew, See and Bassett, to rendezvous training in a simulator at a NASA contractor. They circled in the murk, couldn't see their buddies' jet.

See instead had turned tightly, banked left: he thought he might eyeball the runway. But the ceiling kept dropping. Ahead of him in the airport complex was Building 101: corrugated iron roof, workshop for space capsules. See "broke hard right," "lit his jet's afterburners," tried to climb, but too late.

The starboard wing tore into the building, sparked "a sheet of flame" at the exposed ceiling, scattered debris onto an escape-hatch window in progress. Men dove under benches. The plane skidded to its end on a lot below, "burning furiously."

When Stafford and Cernan landed, they heard the tower ask, *Who was in NASA 901?* Meaning: which set of astronauts just expired.

The White Room where the Gemini 9 capsule sat was undamaged; they'd deliver it to NASA just days later. Stafford and Cernan would fly in it in just over three months.

My grandfather, senior buyer for McDonnell Douglas sitting at his desk, felt the impact. Upstairs, a coworker fought the fire with a hose, waded through water from a broken pipe.

IV.

Richard—he goes by "Dick"—has eight children, my father the oldest. I lingered in his wood-paneled den at the space mementos he kept after retirement, football or golf always on TV, it seemed. He lamented filling that room with cigar smoke, announced on a family float trip that he'd quit, wondered if he'd done it sooner, "maybe we wouldn't have so many ciggy butts around here," my aunts and uncles still smokers.

The sewing kit my mother gave me is housed in a cigar box of his, no longer aromatic. I take after that side of the family, dark hair and eyes, descendants of a French-Canadian fur trader who came south. When we'd gather in the summer for river trips, the nightly bonfire would leave me with a sore throat in the morning.

In my early forties, I spent a week on the beach reading about moon missions, another kind of vastness than the Gulf's, before I realized I should ask my grandfather more about what he'd done.

V.

An attitude control system for Mercury crafts sits somewhere in the Smithsonian. Valves, spacers, and thrusters propelled hydrogen peroxide over a silver screen to stabilize and orient the capsule's pitch, yaw, and roll. Richard Ampleman bought it for the space program.

He also acquired a periscope, "which was delivered but did not fly," he told me, "because the astronauts opted for a window." For Gemini, the middle child, named for its two-man missions, he oversaw eight buyers who procured "tens of millions of dollars" in materials alone, everything needed for the capsules.

I think in particular of the ablative heat shield, wide disc made of silicone that hardened in its honeycomb mold, then changed to gas as the vehicle plunged at seventeen thousand miles per hour, heat from the friction of reentry. The substance vaporized, wicking the worst of the warmth away.

Such a material turns fire against itself, letting the destruction be purposeful. It buffers. One part of a vehicle preserving the rest.

The char structure "is not reusable," the Smithsonian notes. That museum's ablated shield, from the unmanned Gemini 2, looks as pockmarked as the moon. The item description doesn't say what it smells like.

On a moon crater named for a sixteenth-century Jesuit astronomer, there's a twelve-ounce-bottle's worth of water spread through a cubic meter of soil, not enough to drink or drown in. An astronaut on a spacewalk felt water on the back of his head; a *goldfish in a fishbowl,* he lurched back to the airlock, globs of water covering his ears, eyes, nose, in danger of drowning 250 miles from any ocean. Swim class teaches babies to float until a parent can pluck them from the pool. Because bodies of water beckon. My cousin's child was found face down in an in-ground, near the plastic pool he'd asked to play in. In church they get a silver cup of holy water over their heads, startle when it's poured. *We are bathed in the glory of God.* Water rushed through three hundred feet of tubes in Luca Parmitano's spacesuit to keep him from overheating, until some, blocked by a clogged filter, seeped into his air vent. A black hole galaxies away makes water by sucking in material, releasing energy waves that knock H and O together. In a children's movie, a claymation Jesus stands in an unwatery river that folds around his robes. His jaw jerks as he reminisces about playing in the river with his cousin, then he dives underwater, suddenly animated cartoon, pausing beneath the surface as if he knows what will happen when he rises. Luca's station-mates doffed his helmet, wiped more than a liter of water from his face with towels. Exposed to vacuum, water vented into space wouldn't freeze at first; it would boil away, evaporating into a crystal mist. God's dome separated the water below from the water above, and He called the dome *sky*. The water above the firmament is, of course, a mirage, just waves of light scattered by gas molecules. The water below has enough give to cushion the blow of a NASA capsule splashing down from the heavens, enough tension to keep it from sinking.

ALPHA

In the charm quark, in the spark
of a helium ion separated
from its atom, in the arc
of a parabolic flight at its peak,
floating above the stratus,

in the random satin of
a spiral galaxy ages in the past,
the repeating static
of a pulsar, the spasm of
an anthem from an alto

saxophone. In the birthmark
on a babe-in-arms, the stretchmark,
the plasma TV, blood platelets,
plasma from a solar flare
headed for intergalactic

space. In the lattice of
the Van Allen belt corralling
radiation. In the drip of sarcasm,
the defaced sanctuary, the analgesic,
the foretaste of death in the chalky

contrast drink for a CT scan.
In the chasm,
the pockmark, cytoplasm,
the dark wasteland
unveiling the grounding landmark,

the home base, the status update:
all we can fathom,
why we want to be warm,
the angel-herder, the I AM,
all we know by heart.

OMEGA

Earthrise

The slippage between *oh* and awe,
  sound that escapes the larynx as a
    blue pearl crests above a lunar waste-
      land, wreathed in thinnest glow: home,
      celestial scrimshaw from the hands of an
    unknown glassblower, lodestone, jovial host
and transport.

CALAMITY DAYS

Half a billion years ago my current city
was a shallow tropical sea
in the intertidal zone. Its official fossil

is the *Isorophus cincinnatiensis,* edrioasteroid
—a seated star, kin to starfish—
which adhered to shells like a barnacle.

To dine, they opened their five arms
and enclosed their food in an embrace.

/The Kuiper Belt, that donut-shaped
assemblage of solar-system leftovers,
may harbor another planet. I paddled
there to seek it out amid the crullers

and glazed methane-ice rocks. My finger
joints calcified in half-hinge; I felt the draw

of a cavity in space-time, either a planetoid
or black hole; I had to tell them—
it might be the new home we've
been seeking—I set my solar sail

for an about-face, I missed
the smell of petrichor,
I missed my people.

/Wrapped sweaty in my comforter,
I dream incessantly of my hometown
but get confused: Where am I in time?
Where is my husband? My son?

The malleable narrative molds itself,
friends from my twenties convincing me
the shuttle bus will loop around,

surely my family will arrive before the end
of the fireworks show, then we can find
a conventional home in a subdivision.

/Still, my dread of that dark crux was knit
into me, primordial, like my lungs'
ability to take in nitrogen—inert gas
nearly four-fifths of what we breathe—
and send it back out again. Even if

it might be our deliverance
from planetary devastation, I sensed
pure force, evidence of
a malevolent force in the cosmos, should
I tell you again about the disasters?

/There are serotonin receptors in the gut
one doctor explains, and the epigastric rock
just below my sternum finally makes sense.

Sedimentary layers of fiascos and vexations
forming a fossil record of my anxiety.

I want to be clairvoyant, oracle to
suburban parents about which things
are really worth worrying about.

R0, case rates, mask thread-count,
the dust motes rising from a child's
solar plexus, it's hard to know what to pick.

/e.g., (1) The carbonaceous-chondrite
asteroid dropped from the northeast
at 45°, depositing a layer of shocked

quartz in the Yucatan. (2) Pluto's
atmosphere is disappearing as it slides
on its oval ellipse away from the sun.

(3) When our yellow dwarf starts losing
hydrogen, it will burn helium, red giant,

/The state allows schools calamity days
each year, due to weather or local
turmoil—not a lockdown or active-
shooter drill, when bodies are still at desks

or hiding in closets. Power loss, flooding,
fire, chemical leak, lack of teachers:

children still need to be instructed
a particular number of hours.
But leave room for calamity,

leave room for the soothsayers'
warnings and plague-signs like
iguanas dropping frozen from the trees.

and overtake every planet up to Mars.

/The dust on Mars might be toxic.
So don't count on that to be our out.
Hexavalent chromium, calcium
perchlorate: it would get everywhere—

inside the habitat, all over the suits,
and into machinery.

Don't breathe it in (silicosis).
Don't run your fingers
through its grit (thyroid disrupter).

/Pregnant, I dreamed of a blond
four-year-old son, which he became.
When we tried for a second kid,
I wanted to wake and know, so that I didn't

have to unwrap another plastic testing
stick. In that scrim between stillness
and the brain tick-tocking itself awake,

I'd wait for the universe's photons
to nudge neurons into action. I even tried

to write it out like a plot-treatment:
if this, then that. To conjure up a person
through scrawl and scribble.

/On the flight home I thought about
the women on Apollo missions—not
astronauts but centerfolds glued to

window shades and the checklist flipbooks
on spacesuit gloves as pranks. Miss February
in her peach dot matrix was the first woman

to see the moon's far side, to marvel
as the Earth rose, a fervid blue,
above the craters. I'm the next,

but when I tell them I've seen Christa
McAuliffe's crater, their radio-wave replies
sound tinny, voiced by robots,

was I missed, have I been gone too long,
should I not have reminded them
that mothers go missing sometimes?

/My grade-school classmate Kelly vanished
in her thirties from a convenience-store
parking lot, her green eyes selfie-smiling

from posters, have you seen me.
I dream of her dance partner in our gym-
class waltzes, now a Division-I baseball
coach; I have to tell him she didn't

run away, wasn't held against her will,
but fell into a ravine, was ensnarled
in brambles, died from exposure.

Until one night he says that he knows,
I can forget, can wake up, my son
has turned on the light, is asking

what we'll be doing today.

/Kelly's son was ten when she didn't
come home. I don't dream of him,
but my son and I walk the antiquated

hallways of my grade school;
it's uncanny that he's old enough
to attend it, my double, some section

of the psyche set in the past
even as it processes my ongoing
pandemic life, housebound, homesick.

/Upon returning home, I almost didn't
notice the time difference, except that
things weren't where I'd left them.

People I expected to be convivial
were cool; some had moved away.

The constellations had redrawn themselves.
I wasn't a Leo anymore. The baseball
stadium had a mixed-use development
next door: high-end bar, office space.

/Immediately a committee formed
to analyze my findings. Immediately
I felt obsolete, time-ruined,
marred by my nearness to Planet X.

You might expect the rest:
endless delays, partisan grousing,
like a performance-art piece that
repeats a ridiculous foxtrot,

all the dancers in dark glasses,
sunburned eyes from UV rays
off a too-white snowscape,
promenade after turn after
slow-slow-quick-quick,

/Surely I don't miss her enough
to be the one memorializing her,
I hadn't seen her for more than

two decades when she walked into
the fields surrounding Crooked Creek,
I'm just the one typing while
my son asks me to come sit with him,

he can't be alone: even though I don't
share breaking news with him, he asks
when I'm going to die, and I say

I won't, we're going to fly
through space together on this couch
as long as we want to.

we weren't going anywhere.

/We may want to live elsewhere
than the globe we're gnawing at,
but we'll always stay here, imagining

an intergalactic Eden terraformed
to our specifications, as we slurp on
a saltwater martini, pulp the last

of the old-growth into toilet paper.
We don't have enough rare-earth
metals to build a fleet of starships.

We just have the rare Earth: succulent
rainforest, scrumptious estuaries, oxygen
by the lungful. I can't imagine it otherwise.

/Near my birthplace two sizeable rivers
converge. You wouldn't know you'd
reached their confluence because

it looks like just a vaster river. I land on
the same muddy bank each night I fall
asleep, my watch face illegible,

this moment fused with primal flashbacks,
Kelly missing again, my son
demanding my attention, I haven't

visited home in years, I'm there now,
if I travel to the edge of the galaxy
and return, I'll gain time back, I'll get
home, safe haven, no cataclysms.

Acknowledgments

The following poems appeared previously in these literary journals, sometimes in slightly different versions:

32 Poems: "Alpha" and "Birth"; *Colorado Review:* "Point of Departure"; *Cortland Review:* "The Three-Year-Old in the Fertility-Clinic Waiting Room"; *Ecotone:* "'The Future Isn't What It Once Was'"; *Georgia Review:* "Calamity Days"; *Jet Fuel Review:* "Self-Portrait as Laser Inferometer Space Antenna (LISA)" and "Space Pastoral"; *Matter:* "Domestic Concerns" and "A Smack of Jellyfish"; *Meridian:* "Water of Life"; *Miracle Monocle:* "Breaking the Wheel," "Supermommy," and "Try Staying Home"; *Mom Egg Review:* "Unremarkable"; *museum of americana:* "Mae and Nichelle, in Space & on Earth"; *New South:* "Filling in the Pond" and "Public Intimacies"; *Passengers Journal:* "Tenuous Blueprint"; *Presence:* "Barren Trinkets" and "This Is My Body"; *Reformed Journal:* "Godbaby" and "Rotation"; *The Rumpus:* "Mom in Space" and "Stay-at-Home Chronicles"; *Shenandoah:* "Lunar Deceptions"; *The Shore:* "Appropriate Care"; *South Dakota Review:* "Acquiring the Fire"; *Southern Humanities Review:* "Reasons for Lack of Success"; *Southern Review:* "Midden" and "The YouTube Gamers My Son Watches Yell Constantly to Demonstrate Excitement"; *Sweet:* "Venus"; *TAB:* "A/Steroid" and "Autoimmunity and Microgravity."

"Breaking the Wheel" appeared also in *The St. Louis Anthology* (2019) and *New Poetry from the Midwest 2019*.

A book by a working mother with a chronic illness—mostly written during a pandemic, no less—doesn't happen in a vacuum. My greatest thanks to the following, without whom this book would not have come together:

The Institute for Advanced Catholic Studies at USC (especially Father James Heft and Gary Adler), for hosting me and my fellow Generations-in-Dialogue Mullin Scholars, including Dave Griffith, Samuel Martin, Jenny Shank, Kathleen Witkowska Tarr, Brian Volck, Gregory Wolfe, and our guest Martha Serpas; the Ohio Arts Council for its Individual Excellence Award in 2022; and the Hermitage Artist Retreat, a residency that descended like a deus ex machina when I didn't expect it, without which this book would not have been born.

Those who gave feedback on the poems and essays, including Katy Didden, Rebecca Morgan Frank, Rebecca Hazelton, Matt Miller, Sarah Rose Nordgren, Joshua Robbins, and Elizabeth Lindsey Rogers.

Tracy Zeman for the careful first read of the manuscript, and Felicia Zamora for encouraging me to trust my instincts.

Deepest thanks to George David Clark and Cate Lycurgus, workshop-mates who have been companions on the journey. I'm so grateful to have your friendship and insights, and I'm in awe of your own talents.

Some of the content in this book would not have existed without the help of Dr. John Houk, Dr. Krystene DiPaola, and Dr. Julie Rios and the compassion of Dr. Suruchi Thakore and Dr. Emily Hurley in the hardest hours.

The staff at LSU Press, including James W. Long, Neal Novak, and Barbara Neely Bourgoyne: it's excellent to be working with you again.

Those who took care of and educated my son when I was working on this project and others: Rose Hageman, the preschool and kindergarten staff at Saint Aloysius Gonzaga, and the elementary teachers at Saint James.

For general encouragement and lifting of spirits: My colleagues at *The Cincinnati Review,* Acre Books, and the University of Cincinnati. Other space writers and lovers, including the Facebook Space Hipsters group. My family, who supported me as a reader and writer from an early age.

Jeff and Jeremiah, for being the reason there are poems.

And for all of those experiencing the unremarkable sadness of loss and disappointment.

Notes

BOOK EPIGRAPHS

Diane Ackerman's space-opera masterpiece is unfortunately out of print.

My son wants it registered that he doesn't think typing words is boring anymore; in fact, he likes to do it himself sometimes.

POEMS

"Lunar Deceptions" quotes or paraphrases the following: "The Prevalence of Autoimmune Disorders in Women: A Narrative Review" (Fariha Angum et al.) in the journal *Cureus* from May 2020; Virginia Vitzthum, a biological anthropologist quoted in "Menstrual Cycles Intermittently Sync with Moon Cycles: Study" by Asher Jones in *The Scientist* from February 2021; "The Moon's Gravity Does Not Fully Explain How Ocean Tides Work" by Dave Mosher on Business Insider from June 2017; "The Moon Has a Tail, and Earth Wears It Like a Scarf Once a Month" by Brandon Specktor on Live Science from March 2021; "A Breakthrough in the Mystery of Why Women Get So Many Autoimmune Diseases" by Olga Khazan in the *Atlantic* from June 2019; and "In Event of Moon Disaster" memo written by H. R. Haldeman in July 1969, available in the National Archives online.

"Tenuous Blueprint": The epigraph is from Jorie Graham's poem "The Way Things Work," which first appeared in *Hybrids of Plants and of Ghosts* (1980).

"Try Staying Home": Wally Funk was one of thirteen women known as the Mercury 13 who passed all the same medical tests required of potential astronauts in the early 1960s. Though the women weren't accepted by NASA because they couldn't have served as test pilots, Wally Funk later flew in space in 2021, with Jeff Bezos's Blue Origin suborbital spacecraft.

Valentina Ponomaryova is quoted in "The First Woman in Space," a podcast episode in the BBC *Space* series, originally broadcast in June 2013.

The scene with Pat White in Susan Borman's living room for the Apollo 8 launch is available in Part Two of the 2019 documentary *Chasing the Moon* in PBS's American Experience series. The first American man in space, Alan Shepard, impatient after hours of delays before launch, told the mission team to "fix your little problem and light this candle."

The epigraph to the Ralph Abernathy section is from "For the Poor People's Campaign, the Moonshot Was Less Than a Triumph" by Imani Perry in the *New York Times* from July 16, 2019. Other details, including the words on a protest sign and NASA Administrator Tom Paine's exchange with Abernathy are available in "NASA Chief Briefs Abernathy after Protest at Cape" in the UPI Archives from July 16, 1969. A retrospective article ("Apollo 11 Launch VIPs Included LBJ, Charles Lindbergh, Johnny Carson and Thousands More") by Roger Simmons in the Orlando Sentinel from July 2, 2019, includes this paragraph:

> Witnessing the launch seemed to temper Abernathy's opposition. "For that particular moment and second, I really forgot the fact that we have so many hungry people in the United States of America," Abernathy said afterward. "I was one of the proudest Americans as I stood on this soil, on this spot. I think it's really holy ground and it will be more holy once we feed the hungry and care for the sick and provide for those who don't have houses."

"You are but a mist that appears for a little while and then vanishes" is in the Christian Bible, James 4:14.

Details about Anna and Kristin Fisher's experiences are available in transcripts from the NASA Johnson Space Center Oral History Project interviews of Anna Fisher, especially the one conducted by Jennifer Ross-Nazzal on March 3, 2011.

The launch described in the Karen Nyberg section is the SpaceX Crew Dragon Demo-2 flight on May 30, 2020 (though I've cheated a bit: she wore the handkerchief dress for a scrubbed launch on May 27). The local paper mentioned there is the *Houston Chronicle,* specifically the article "NASA Family out of This World" by Eric Berger from November 8, 2013, which also contains Doug Hurley's response. (See the notes for "Water of Life" for more about Karen Nyberg.)

The final lines in the poem are from "A Rocket Launch Can't Unite Us until the Space World Acknowledges Our Divisions" by Loren Grush on The Verge from June 3, 2020.

"Rotation" includes an image inspired by "The Helical Model—Our Solar System Is a Vortex," an animation posted on YouTube on August 24, 2012, by DjSadhu.

"Secondary Infertility" ascribes to the main character a sentence said by astronaut Dave Scott during Apollo 15.

"Supermommy" quotes *The Space Station: A Personal Journey* (1987) by Hans Mark.

"Neil and Me and Work and the Body" describes a *60 Minutes* interview of Neil Armstrong from 2005. The journalist is Ed Bradley. The essay also quotes a personal email from Richard Ampleman from February 2020 and *First Man: The Life of Neil A. Armstrong* (2018 reissue) by James R. Hansen, and it makes reference to "Apollo Lunar Astronauts Show Higher Cardiovascular Disease Mortality: Possible Deep Space Radiation Effects on the Vascular Endothelium" by Michael D. Delp et al. in *Scientific Reports* from July 2016.

"Autoimmunity and Microgravity" describes the experiences of astronaut Scott Kelly, who spent 340 days in space. He recounts his experience in *Endurance: My Year in Space, A Lifetime of Discovery* (2017).

"A/Steroid": Destiny O. Birdsong's poem "Auto-immune" (with the repeated end-word "syringe") is available in *Negotiations* (2020).

"The Shade on Mercury (Ailey Crater)": Mercury's Ailey crater was named in 2012. "Move, Members, Move" is the final movement of Alvin Ailey's *Revelations*. Performances by the Alvin Ailey American Dance Theater are available on YouTube, including at https://www.youtube.com/watch?v=RrPJ4kt3a64&t=3s starting at 23:11.
"Menace and funk" is how Alvin Ailey described *Revelations* in his auto-biography of the same name, written with A. Peter Bailey (1995). The quote from Ailey in the final stanza is from a video once posted on the website of the Alvin Ailey American Dance Theater.

"Mae & Nichelle, in Space & on Earth": The experiment in the first section was described in "Space Shuttle Experiment Shows Frogs Can Reproduce in Space" by Paul Recer from the Associated Press on March 13, 1995. The NASA recruitment video described in the second section is available online at https://www.youtube.com/watch?v=Lca9_EDMcX0. Many of that section's other details, including the quote from Martin Luther King, Jr., are from Nichols's autobiography *Beyond Uhura: Star Trek and Other Memories* (1994). The quote in the fourth section ("grabs her left hand . . .") is from the article "Ex-Astronaut Jemison Accuses Cop of Brutality" by Gary Borg in the *Chicago Tribune* from March 1, 1996. The final section quotes "Girls Ask Dr. Mae Jemison about Space," posted to *Good Morning America*'s YouTube channel on May 23, 2018: https://www.youtube.com/watch?v=JZoDnBoTTxQ.

"Stay-at-Home Chronicles": The details about the romaine leaves are from Scott Kelly's book *Endurance: My Year in Space, A Lifetime of Discovery* (2017).

"Space Flora and Fauna": The quote in the epigraph is from Scott Kelly's book *Endurance: My Year in Space, A Lifetime of Discovery* (2017). The quote in the twelfth stanza is from Neil deGrasse Tyson's *Astrophysics for People in a Hurry* (2017). The "one of you" in the fifteenth and sixteenth stanza is astronaut Bob Behnken, speaking at a press conference after he and Doug Hurley returned home on Crew Dragon Demo-2 in August 2020.

"Midden": This poem and "Breaking the Wheel" describe the ongoing fire at the Bridgeton Landfill and the remaining radioactive material from the Manhattan Project in the West Lake Landfill. Wikipedia described a midden as "debris of human activity." The poem also quotes "The Bridgeton Landfill Fire, Explained" by David Bodamer on the Waste 360 website, and "Something's Burning" from the *Earth Island Journal* online in Spring 2016.

"The Future Isn't What It Once Was": The speech by Neil Armstrong appeared in a Cincinnati Museum Center exhibit, *Destination Moon,* as described in the poem. This experience was one of the main triggers for this book's project.

The poem also references "Tree Rings Show No Warming Tendency," an Associated Press article from May 21, 1993; "Summer 2012 Brought Record-Breaking Melt to Greenland" by Michon Scott from Climate.gov on December 5,

2012; and "A 40-Year-Old Mystery about Rising Temperatures on the Moon Has Been Solved—and It Was Probably the Apollo Astronauts' Fault" by Hilary Brueck on the Business Insider site on June 12, 2018.

"Acquiring the Fire": The quote in the first section is from "7 Common Space Myths Debunked by Actual Astronauts and Science" by Christopher McFadden on the Interesting Engineering site on January 11, 2019.

The quotes in the second section are from Apollo 9 transcripts and also repeated in Gene Cernan's autobiography, *The Last Man on the Moon: Astronaut Eugene Cernan and America's Race in Space* (1999), with Don Davis.

The quotes in the third section are from "'A Bad Call': The Accident Which Almost Lost Project Gemini" by Ben Evans, on the AmericaSpace site from March 5, 2012, and "Losing the Moon" by W. Pate McMichael from *St. Louis Magazine* online on July 28, 2006.

The Mercury attitude control system in the final section is pictured at https://learninglab.si.edu/resources/view/23121. My grandfather's quotes are from a personal email on February 20, 2020. The Gemini 2 heat shield is pictured at https://airandspace.si.edu/collection-objects/heat-shield-gemini/nasm_A197818 14000.

"Water of Life": Luca Parmitano's space walk occurred on July 16, 2013. His quote is from an interview soon after, while he was still on Station. A fascinating account of his experience is available in a BBC recording online, "I Nearly Drowned in Space," originally broadcast December 14, 2015. Karen Nyberg, also featured in the poem "Try Staying Home," is one of the station-mates helping towel off his face. The hymn phrase is from "River of Glory" by Dan Schutte. The children's movie described is *The Miracle Worker* from 2000. This poem is in memory of my second cousin, Ryan Chamberlain.

"Calamity Days/Upon Returning Home": This poem references DryDredgers. org on "Cincinnati's Official Fossil" at http://drydredgers.org/isorophus.htm and quotes a Mars Exploration Program Analysis's Group report on "Toxic Effects of Martian Dust on Humans" (available at https://mepag.jpl.nasa.gov/goal.cfm ?goal=5).

Printed in the USA
CPSIA information can be obtained
at www.ICGtesting.com
CBHW031157220524
8864CB00015B/104